Smoke and Ash

Swirling smoke like the swirling
memories in her head
dance with the air around her.
The burning paper like her burning desire
to be free.
But like the paper that turns to ash,
she is smothered and
only the burnt remnants of the cigarette
and her life remain.

Prayer Girl

A statue kneels on my dresser
with folded hands and understanding eyes.
She believes, she asks, and she prays
Each night I wonder why?

Didn't she witness
what was all around?
In my childhood room,
there was no hope to be found.

A girl in her closet crying
with fear.
A piece of her identity stolen
with each tear.

The yelling grew louder
and darkness crept in.
There was no escape.
She grew up to be him.

Shadows in My Soul

The shadows that dance in my soul
are not the shadows you see as I move through this life.
The ones...on the walls that dance in your arms,
the ones on the ground that dance around laughter and flames.

These shadows stir up
like bottom feeders in sand.
These shadows are no shadows at all.
They are today, only who I am.

First Anxiety

Paralyzing fear rips me from my sleep.
Below, “I’m Just a Girl” plays with intensity-
beats thump along with my pulsating heart.

You are not just a girl! You
are a lifelong disaster that lives within me
and dances with the shadows in my heart.

Hiding in my Closet

At 36, I should not do this anymore, but
you guard me against the shadows in my heart
that spin deep within.

I am an adult now, I have my own home
my own closet, my own safety, and yet
fear tears at me
from the closet I get pushed back to-
the one from that home, that
distant home that won't let me go.

Through my closet here, I am transferred there
Curled up on the floor, back against the door
Because shadows can't find you in the dark.

True Pandemic

In the grips of active addiction, I
was never more lonely
surrounded by people who loved me.

I found ways to avoid going home, excuses
to drink, reasons to escape.
Darker and darker my world became and I
was the one making it that way.

In that dark time
working from home was the new norm.
A pandemic was raging outside, and I
became trapped in the one place I
felt I did not belong.

Fulltime employee
Mom turned teacher
Husband as coworker
Masked faces
More isolation

Wash the dishes. Answer emails. Attend a virtual meeting.
Drink a glass of wine.
Numb the pain, the distant images of a past prison
Empty the trash. Make dinner. Teach a child to read.
Converse with husband.
Drink another glass.
The day's half over, then I can have more.

Wake up. Do it again.
No separation from one
to the next.
Drink one more.
Drink one more.

Watching My Son

In his head, which
is his world, dinosaurs
come alive.
They take him to places
Jurassic and
wild.

In my head, which
is my world, demons
come alive.
They take me to places
past and
chaotic.

I want to stop
my demons from becoming
wild in his mind
protect him
from a world that is a
real-life Jurassic Park where
survival is the only way to exist.

Snakes at the Pool

They teased me
And told me the
Fence around the pool was
To keep snakes
Out.
What they didn't tell me was
About the snake
Hidden within disguised
As a friend.

His fingers worked like snakes
On my body
Every throw a little deeper
Innocence exploding with every splash
Plunging my spirit beneath the surface
Until I rose again
To be thrown again

And then I realize the
Fence was there
To keep me in.

The Snake's Return

A familiar feeling,
the snakes
that invaded my innocence
returned.

We traded the fenced-in pool
for my parent's living room couch.
His lips and fingers raced across my body.
long last tension released.

It was love, I naively thought
after all the years since those first
snake-like touches.
But it felt like the pool again.
Like ice-cold water swirling around
my head and
this time when I emerged,
the gate was open
and he let me out.

Inside her Head

The window of her therapist's
Office sits high and horizontal
On the wall, only
the blue and
Clouds of white visible, she
looks to
Escape,
To go back to her safe
Space- the mountains.

Near a waterfall, the
cool mist dances among
the stones beneath her, and
Negative ions bring
Peace and life to her
Tired body.

The therapist brings her deeper and deeper noticing how she feels.
13 again and crying in
Her closet
There was no waterfall there
Only his face
and a door.

Addiction is...

Addiction is getting a high from the anticipation of that next bitter sip
Addiction is shaky hands reaching for the first one of the day
Addiction is empty bottles crashing in the garbage can and everyone knowing without you saying a word
Addiction is desperation for the cure that you are not able to find
Addiction is emptiness and a longing to be free from the agonies of the mind
Addiction is disappointment in their eyes as you make promises you cannot keep
Addiction is one choice at a time until there is no longer that choice

Editing a Life

She writes the **abstract**
of her life, filled with **boilerplates**
that never change, and begins with
the **bastard title** that summarizes her
pain.

There is no **art** in her book, but
plenty of **back matter** to explain any
AA-Author's Alteration. But it isn't
the right kind of AA for this story.
Hers is a meeting and a number
of days since she last
tried to escape like the **air** on
her pages- white spaces to
be left blank.

Pulling Myself Out

I sit and watch and play and fight
images in my mind, they run and leap
on past reality toward my night-
mares that border my sanity and keep
me from living with peace and hope today.
I cannot be free to live and love
and laugh, but only to listen- they say
listen to my words of lies, my words of
criticism and angry hate.
Living this way drains my heart and soul,
I must remove myself from this fate
to grow and to dream and become a whole
person, a whole self that creates and thrives
in a world that walks with other lives.

Addiction Diamond

The diamond ring I wear reminds me I am sliding on black ice trying to avoid the one imperfection on the surface, because this imperfection is me.
Imperfect mother,
imperfect wife,
imperfect woman.

The black diamond I wear is held between two perfect stones, translucent and pure.
But I sit raised in the center and reminds me that I am alone.
Alone in my darkness,
alone in my addiction,
alone in my despair.

The black diamond ring I wear frightens me,
because it means that I am loved.

Recovery Diamond

Surrounded by two white stones,
a black diamond sits on my hand and glistens
as I move through my day and our life.
He placed it on my hand with vows eternal.
Its one imperfection reminds me perfect does not exist.
No perfect wife,
no perfect woman,
no perfect mother to our children.
Only me
like the uniqueness of the black diamond and our love.

Human Doings

Swirls of pinks, yellows, blues, and grays rise from the water to the endless sky as people walk the dock, navigation in hand- only the destination in mind. Dolphins playfully poke their thin noses from beneath and they snap bright flashes of their environment. Only through a lens, they view their world. They don't even take notice that she is in their shots. The girl standing, hands on her face, eyes wide open, screaming. No one stops, no one speaks to her. She screams louder, falls to her knees and no one sees her misery. Ding! A message received. Swoosh! A message sent. But no one messages her, the screaming girl on her knees beneath their devices. Kindness is no longer in existence, only images on the tiny screens they hold capture their attention. As they continue to pass by, she continues to scream, lost in reality, and they, lost in a world of doing rather than being.

A Thought

There is something about burning
Paper to ash falling freely, only to
be captured by its container.

Bright embers glow in the dark,
and it is put out.

Save Me Tea

Peppermint tea helps me breathe. It opens my stomach and allows me to stand tall. It relaxes my muscles and clears my mind. The fresh scent entrances my nostrils and lifts my head to a higher place like a balloon floating gently in the breeze. I wish peppermint tea could lift me from my past. Make my parents capable of love, compassion, and kindness - toward me, toward themselves. Then these wounds would be healed and I would finally know what it is like to be free.

Bartender

The bar is empty again, but
it won't be for long. The
door will open
she'll sign in, leaving
her blurry signature and number, so
no one knows she was here. 89-
like the number of times, she's striving
for to sit at the corner stool and order a third.
It's always a third.
It only takes two, but I pour her
a third.

During her first pour, the familiar blue-collar man approaches,
smelling already of beer and disappointment. He'll go for
the brown liquor- beer hasn't been enough for
what feels like day eight of his week. There is no
separation of time for him- only hard work, a small paycheck,
and trying to escape enough to do it again
tomorrow.

On to her second, and the teacher arrives
right on cue.
She understands his language. He orders
an IPA and they toast to the students because
if it weren't for them, he'd quit.

With her final pour, the CrossFit crew comes in,

glistening with sweat and donning the latest
fashion in activewear. They look around and
feel superior because *they* worked out before
coming in. But they still came in.

It's time for her to leave, before
her husband gets home from work, now
ready to put on her wife and mother disguise
she wears with a strain.
The door opens and she passes more patrons
coming in with more
reasons to drink.

He's Gone

A familiar tune emerged
from her phone.
The song that they danced to
in the gazebo when he had finally made his way back to her
in their new home.
She continued to pick up toys, clothes, and dishes
that were left from the nightly chaos of three boys.
Who was calling and
why hadn't she changed her ringtone?

Day 111

1 attend a meeting, remembering that relapse is a part of recovery
2 make the kids lunches, feeling grateful for the task
3 wake the kids up, being present in the moment
4 take the kids to school, embracing the day ahead
5 begin work, enduring any challenges that arise
6 Pick up the kids, being present in the moment
7 Practice the piano, creating new habits
8 Make dinner, filling the body with nutrients
9 Go to bed, reflecting on the day

Each day I survive, confined
by the counting.

Not by Blood, But by Choice

Through a broken path you
And I were joined.
Together we fight
the demons of an addicted life.
She could not pull out of hers
like you pulled me back out of mine.
You are my purpose to heal, to love,
to remain whole

You call her mom, but I will wake with you
when the nightmares come.
I will cheer from the sidelines.
I will strengthen you as you grow.
Not by blood, but by choice
you are my son.

Deciding to Live

Lurking behind the doctors, I saw the shadows.
They were there all day hiding behind our laughter.
They waited patiently to take one or both of us.
They tried and failed that day, but took me after.
They followed us home and lurked through the house.
They hung over the bed as we slept.
They would not let me escape.

I fell to my demons.
One...two...three years I fell.
I fell until I couldn't see through my broken lenses.
Blinded, I had nothing to lose.
I stepped through the darkness where the shadows could not follow.

Let Me Fall

Dried leaves beneath my feet crunch each dark place from my past. No longer on the path to hell, I rake and burn them to ash. Keep falling away leaves, from the base that held you for so long. Drop to the earth knowing your time is done. Winter is coming to further solidify your death. The world will be washed in icy whiteness. I will glide along the surface knowing you are beneath me where you belong, and cannot return. Let me fall and let me rise with spring's rebirth.

Make Room for Me

Make room in my heart, Lord.
Move whatever needs moving
to expand the space within.
Bring to the front what I cannot see-
a love true and whole for me.

One to Live

It is well with me
that I have fallen and risen,
slipped and stood up again.
I know the hurt it caused.
I know the anger it brought. I also
know the love it strengthened and
the will it created in me.
No longer a will to survive, but
one to live.

Recovery Girl

With her alarm set, she rests her head knowing that she will wake to recovery. 3:45 AM she gathers herself from the sheets and moves through the dark house, weaving her way through the obstacles of toys left from her children's play. For a time there is no chaos, noise, or needing. She is able to listen as she pours water into a glass. On her porch, she is welcomed by the early morning air. It enters her lungs like being greeted by an old friend. With a few taps on her phone, she is in the meeting surrounded by wise friends along equal paths- scattered across the world and never meeting in person, yet all similar in their design. A few readings and the meditation begins. She breathes in peace and breathes out a smile on repeat until her thoughts are no more. She lives between the breaths now, opening herself to her true existence- the one behind the thoughts of who she is. Stepping back into the safety of the space, she reads from the text, dancing with each word. She listens intently to what others have to say with wise understanding and compassion, and she knows what to share. That she sent her addiction out into the world through words held on a page, and not that she isn't that girl anymore, but that she just is now and can continue to be.

www.ingramcontent.com/pod-product-compliance
Lightning Source LLC
LaVergne TN
LVHW012034160826
845678LV00013B/2594

* 9 7 9 8 3 7 4 2 9 8 5 9 8 *